MEDITATIONS
With
MERTON

— 🌿 —

MEDITATIONS
With
MERTON

— ✤ —

Nicki Verploegen

Wipf & Stock
PUBLISHERS
Eugene, Oregon

Wipf and Stock Publishers
199 W 8th Ave, Suite 3
Eugene, OR 97401

Meditations With Merton
A collage of Scripture quotes, original prayers, and Merton's own words
By Verploegen, Nicki
Copyright©1993 by Verploegen, Nicki
ISBN: 1-59752-984-2
Publication date 9/27/2006
Previously published by Liguori, 1993

Scripture texts used in this work are taken from the NEW AMERICAN BIBLE © 1991, 1986, 1970 by the Confraternity of Christian Doctrine, 3211 Fourth Street, N.E., Washington, D.C., and are used with permission. All rights reserved.

Excerpts from *Conjectures of a Guilty Bystander* by Thomas Merton, copyright © 1968, Doubleday & Co., New York, New York, are used with permission.

Excerpts from *New Seeds of Contemplation* by Thomas Merton, copyright © 1972, New Directions Publishing Corporation, New York, New York, are used with permission. In the British Commonwealth, copyright by Anthony Clarke Books, Wheathampstead, Hertfordshire, England.

CONTENTS

Preface	v
I. Personal Integrity	1
II. Sanctity of Life	11
III. Seeds of Identity	23
IV. Integration	35
V. The God Within	47
VI. Labor	59
VII. Solidarity and Service	71
VIII. Words of God	85
IX. God's Will	93
X. Love Is a Foundation	101

PREFACE

On December 10, 1968, America lost one of its most formidable social critics and spiritual leaders. Thomas Merton, a Cistercian monk, died while on pilgrimage in Bangkok, Thailand. Merton, who prior to his death wrote from his hermitage in Kentucky's Abbey of Gethsemani, gained a unique perspective partially aided by the distance that his monastic life afforded him. His incisive and voluminous writings spanned a whole range of topics and contemporary concerns that had rarely been addressed from a monastic vantage point.

Despite the protection of the walls of Gethsemani, "Father Louis," as he was known among his confreres, was far from insular. He wrote passionately about controversial events and dynamics in the twentieth century, including the war in Vietnam, industrialization, nuclear technology, and mass media. His tremendous concern with peace, lived out personally and communally, was articulated at a time of great turmoil in the Western world. His voice was prophetic, both challenging and compelling, as many other prophets have been.

We honor the memory and wisdom of Thomas Merton by looking at what he spoke to all of us about our daily lives. His central concern was the transformation of the human person in intimate relationship with God. Merton was deeply concerned with the underriding spiritual yearning of every human heart, both inside and outside the monastery. He was tuned in to the interior journey the traveler walks in a troubled world that often hampers the transcendent hunger for God and for more than functional accomplishments.

This process was apparent in his approach to subjects that appeal to people in their everyday life in a working world. While believing that prayer was primary, Merton wove his message and challenge to deal with many topics that people today hunger for guidance on.

This book is an attempt to reflect on his words in light of everyday living. I have taken the liberty of interpreting some of Merton's statements in a broader context than they may have originally been written. I pray that there is no misrepresentation of his foundational approach in my expansion. Since an individual's knowledge is always limited, however, I welcome the dialogue that could come in the questioning of my interpretations.

I will look at a series of themes, such as personal integrity, sanctity, identity, integration, labor, God, solidarity, and service and tease out of them Merton's insights that are still valid today. To stimulate meditation, short passages from Merton's works are tied in with a related Scripture passage and an original prayer. I hope this collage of reflections will provide many moments with Merton as your guide.

I welcome the opportunity to share a portion of the great literature and insight that Thomas Merton left the world. He is a significant religious and social figure of the postmodern age, but his words have a perennial quality that will stand the test of time.

We honor this man's contribution to Christianity and to world peace. We hope that those who are hungry for God's voice in their lives will hear it in this compilation and expansion of one man's words and that their own voice will be evoked to speak likewise of God.

Nicki Verploegen

The Hunger in Thomas Merton: Who Was He?

There is hunger in the world. For what are we hungry? Bread for our bodies is a continual issue for many people in a world where three fourths of the Earth's population still struggles for a basic subsistence of food, water, clothing, shelter, and security.

We hunger also on the personal level for fulfillment. We want to see the work of our hands produce something, the ideas of our minds be valued, and the questions of our souls find meaning. We want to contribute to a larger reality than our own narrow, individual existence. We want that sense of accomplishment that gives us potency in the world.

We hunger for relationships, those that connect us on many planes and in many times with humanity. We seek a sense of continuity with our ancestors, whose stories teach us how to avoid some of life's pitfalls. These primordial voices from our past are the heritage that connects us to a larger body of humanity to whom we are indebted. We treasure those relationships in the present through which we know friendship, whether a soul mate who glimpses the profundity of our uniqueness or an acquaintance with whom we laugh, work, and celebrate. Though distance may separate us from these partners in the journey, we continue to admire and appreciate them because their intimacy, courage, and communion with us merit a special regard in our hearts. We also hunger in anticipation of our own progeny, the future generations who will continue the historical process unleashed since humans first defined time. Our hopes for ourselves may not be realized, but we invest those who come after us with the same charge to make it better than we ourselves inherited.

In all of this, we hunger for God. We seek to connect with what is beyond our empirical selves, a Being who orders existence, even if we are not sure how. We live at the edge of the Mystery we call by many names, perceiving God's nearness and magnetism that both draws us and confounds us.

We are hungry. That hunger is a natural part of our human condition. Our incompleteness is the sense of emptiness that moves us to seek God, the One who is hidden but who wants us hungry enough to reach out in response and desire for the Sacred. If we were full, we would see no need for God. Our fullness would hinder our recognition of our need for the mystery of God. Instead, the hunger within us intensifies our search for intimacy and compels us to transcend our selfishness in order to enter into community with God and with others. Paradoxically, the desert in our heart is the fertile ground for the presence of God to manifest in us and through us.

Thomas Merton knew what it was to be spiritually hungry. His writings are filled with the hunger for life, for justice, and for God. At the center of his thought, this hunger revealed itself in the fundamental movement from the false self to the true self. Merton's own life reflects the movement from a life revolving around false suns, distractions, and preferences to a reorientation in an orbit around the Son of God, Jesus Christ. Through a gradual conversion, which eventually led to Roman Catholicism and monasticism, he sought the true self in himself, authored by the Mystery of God and coaxed forward each day into greater intimacy.

He lived a life not unlike many others have lived. Born in France in 1915, two years before the Russian Revolution, he grew up in a single-parent home with a mobile lifestyle. When he was six years old, his American mother died of cancer, leaving him to be cared for by his father, an itinerant artist from New Zealand, and a mix of English and American relatives. He was sent to boarding school, first in France and then in England, where he endured lonely times in his childhood. When he was sixteen, his father died of a brain tumor, and his "orphan" existence was exacerbated. From earliest years, Thomas exhibited the rebellious streak of a misfit who felt estranged in an ever-shifting world.

While touring Italy, however, the eighteen-year-old Merton became fascinated with the churches of Rome and began to make the connection between them and the living Christ. His romance with Christianity solidified when he experienced a gripping vision of his deceased father and knew in a flash his own brokenness. The combination led to his baptism in New York City at the age of twenty-three.

Intrigued by the interior voyage as well as with worldly involvement, Merton continued his bacchic lifestyle as a student at Columbia University. Gradually, he weaned himself from his raucous living when he took a teaching position at St. Bonaventure's in Olean, New York. He was torn between doing social work in Harlem with Catherine de Hueck or becoming a priest. It was not a simple discernment for him. He looked at the Franciscan community, yet desired a true monastic life. He began in earnest to fashion a life of prayer and meditation for himself before making a commitment to the Trappists.

World War II fanned his hatred for war, and in the wake of the conflicts in Europe, his alienation flared all the more. Finally, on December 10, 1941, three days after the bombing of Pearl Harbor Thomas Merton entered Our Lady of Gethsemani Abbey in Kentucky at age twenty-seven, never expecting to leave her walls. Within days after entry he wrote his first letter, exuberant about his new home, the only "home" he had ever walked into and felt so at ease. While in upcoming years he would struggle with the system and authorities in that "home," he recognized in his personality the need for this structure that could anchor him.

Exactly twenty-seven years later on December 10, 1968, Merton would die in Bangkok, half a world away from his monastery home. A contemplative hunger similar to that which had brought him into contemplative communion had taken him to the Orient as an intermonastic contemplative in dialogue with Christian, Buddhist, and Hindu monks. Half of his fifty-four years had been lived in the arms of the world and the other half within the cloister, a tangible display of the twofold engagement with the world and the interior to which he felt drawn.

His concern for the larger world never left him, despite his initial years of "retreat" in formation with the Cistercians. His interior journey toward peace and his creative urges would again lead him back into publishing, sharing his insights with a broader base of readers beyond the monastic community of Gethsemani. For Merton, the theme of inner peace was matched in importance with that of the enfleshment of peace in the world. His initial works focused on the contemplative hunger of the human heart, but these would gradually externalize themselves again in a social critique of technological culture and its alienating effects on the hungry heart. He would embrace the classics of his Western Christian tradition and then at the end of his life expand his horizons to the Eastern religious traditions of Hinduism and Buddhism, most specifically to Zen.

Merton, like all of us, was shaped by the world of his time. He wrote in his autobiography, *Seven Storey Mountain*, "Free by nature in the image of God, I was nevertheless the prisoner of my own violences and my own selfishness, in the image of the world into which I was born." But underlying the specifics of the era he grew up in, his longing for the mystery of God led him to transcend the limitations of his world and move into a margin of wisdom from which he could address all people. While some of his works speak most precisely to professional contemplatives, Merton did not see these writings to be exclusive to vowed religious. Rather, he invites all human beings who seek truth, authenticity, and the mystery of God in intimate union to walk with him in his words and venture into this beauty.

I.
PERSONAL INTEGRITY

The Mystery of Myself

> "To live well myself means for me to know and appreciate something of the mystery of myself: that which is incommunicable, which is at once myself and not myself....If I can understand something of myself and something of theirs, I can begin to share with them the work of building the foundations for spiritual unity."
>
> *Conjectures of a Guilty Bystander*, 95

It is amazing how hard it is to live a healthy, reflective life in the midst of the "normal" chaos of our everyday schedules. It is terribly easy to forget the "mystery of myself" when the demands of the functional world require quick and efficient responses.

The "mystery of myself" is a quiet miracle that requires a focused, gentle presence to someone who often gets overlooked in the juggling of work, children, responsibilities, and the needs of others—one's self. Rarely are we given permission to take time for the appreciation of our own preciousness.

Thomas Merton says this precious "mystery of myself" is "incommunicable." There are very few words that express the totality of a person's uniqueness. That uniqueness is a radiation of the image of God in the flesh of a human person, remarkable in its distinctness. No two chromosomes are the same, scientists tell us. Each collection of cells in each individual human body is specific to that special human being. So the "mystery of myself" is hard to understand and put into words in its very depths.

Merton says this mystery is, paradoxically, at "once myself," deeply part of me but also "not myself." God's manifestation is manifold. The divine impression of God within me is not exclusive to me. God's fullness within me extends beyond my inner self to shine uniquely through the eyes of those other human "mysteries" I meet in everyday life.

I could spend the rest of my life pondering this mystery of self and never fully comprehend it. But in that little understanding, I am called to act. As a human being I have the power to choose to reach out beyond my own life and touch the life in others. Their uniqueness is as profound as my own. There is something common between us in our humanness, even while we remain amazingly different.

From this foundation of spiritual unity, I can call another "sister" or "brother." I can call her or him "friend." I, as a human being, can relate to another as a reflective mystery in her or his own right. Thus, I celebrate the mystery of another as I reverence my own.

Christ shines uniquely in each human face. Icon painters in the Eastern Christian tradition painted pictures of Christ with eyes that were like "windows to heaven." Through them we glimpse holiness and are reminded of God's presence to us.

We are like living icons in the streets, reminding one another of the fantastic creativity of God expressing itself in incredibly diverse combinations. From this uniqueness and commonality, we can share with the Spirit in the building of the kingdom. We can live well, appreciating the miracle of self in union with God and others.

> O Lord, our Lord,
>> how awesome is your name through all the earth!
>
> You have made them little less than a god,
>> crowned them with glory and honor.
>>> Psalm 8:2, 6

— ❦ —

Beloved Creator, I rush so fast that I forget your mysterious beauty in my life. I forget to treasure the uniqueness within me and within those near me. Awaken the eyes of my heart to recognize your face in those I meet today. Give me a fresh willingness to share myself in the building of unity and peace in our world.

Because We Want to Be

> "We believe not because we want to know, but because we want to be. And supernatural faith responds to the mystery of that natural faith which is the core and center of our personal being, the will to be ourselves that is the heart of our natural identity. The higher faith is the will not only to be ourselves, but to find ourselves truly in Christ by obedience to His Father."
>
> *Conjectures of a Guilty Bystander*, 19

There is a mystery about human existence. We are the only beings as far as we know who can reflect on what it is to live, on what it is to be. Something in us makes us want "to be" as fully as possible. We might say that this yearning to be originates in our innate desire to move beyond what we know in our heads to a greater awareness and capacity in our spirits.

We also sense, somewhat vaguely at times, that we are part of a bigger reality beyond human knowledge. If we choose to develop this awareness, we move into faith. What we seek and what we trust is not a tangible, scientifically verifiable fact but an intuitive, elusive, very real part of the whole picture. The mystery of God cannot be researched under a microscope, but we still sense God's existence and participation in our lives.

Most of us know that we would not exist without God's existence. For life itself, we are dependent on a force greater than ourselves with which we are in relationship. This greater Being enables us to be. If we choose, we can enter into deeper awareness of that relationship and unleash significant capacities which without faith we could not possibly realize. In other words, we can become more fully who we are through faith. Our desire, "the will to be ourselves that is the heart of our natural identity," as Merton writes, is found in obedient relationship to the Creator.

Obedience is a much maligned term. To be liberated from its slavish connotations, we must recognize that its root word, *obedire*, means "listening." Obedience is an attentive listening to the Spirit in a relational way. Our conviction of faith tells us that the Spirit wants all good for us and through attentive listening and responding we can realize the good that God wants for us. We can "not only be ourselves but find ourselves truly in Christ by obedience to His Father."

The challenge is to willingly develop the careful art of listening to that higher Power and respond creatively to it. This is not always easy amid the ambiguities of everyday life or in major decision making. We frequently will have to live in the cacophony of inner voices and noise from our world that may make it difficult to decipher the true voice of God. But we believe that if our hearts are yearning for the voice of God, we will be guided. This voice will teach us about "the core and center of our being."

Keep me safe, O God;
>   in you I take refuge.
I say to the LORD,
>   you are my Lord,
>   you are my only good.

I bless the LORD who counsels me;
>   even at night my heart exhorts me.
I keep the LORD always before me;
>   with the Lord at my right,
>   I shall never be shaken.
>>   PSALM 16:1-2, 7-8

— 🌿 —

O Great Being, I want to be fully who I am. I want to see the smile of your face and know that what I am coming to be is what you have created me to be. It is hard for me to listen. There are so many distractions in my life. Teach me the art of obedient listening today for five minutes. Give me a brief time of one-to-one intimacy with you and help me to hear your voice and know your pleasure.

Truest Solitude

> "The truest solitude is not something outside you, not an absence of men or of sound around you; it is an abyss opening up in the center of your own soul."
>
> *New Seeds of Contemplation,* 80

No matter what our vocational call in life is, we all carry a primordial solitude that is unique to us. No one can truly touch this exclusive part of our being except God. We may feel a certain aloneness in this private space, but it is the emptiness of this space that allows for God's centrality in our lives.

We frequently associate loneliness with solitude. We may point out times when we were alone and felt isolated or separated from other people. This is not the solitude Thomas Merton is speaking of. Rather, he is speaking of the deepest abyss of our being where we live in nakedness with the immanent God. The emptiness in our own interior allows for the dwelling of God.

This is the uncomfortable part. It's not easy to live with emptiness. Contemplatives on the journey of interior quiet know how easy it is to fill the void with words or thoughts. But words or thoughts, no matter how holy, intrude upon the mind's focus on God. Our solitude gets congested with escapes that make it easier for us to forget God.

It's not easy to sit quietly in the presence of even a congenial and amiable person. To sit in the presence of a silent God is even more difficult, but it is in this silent abyss that God directs our heart, filling it and forming it according to the unique design God has in mind.

We collaborate with God on this filling and forming process when we give ourselves time to move into true solitude. Getting accustomed to solitude takes some discipline. In many ways, it goes against the cultural trends of our day. But gradually, the quiet of God begins to speak and direct us, and our heart becomes more finely tuned to the frequency that God uses to speak to us.

Initially, solitude can only be felt when alone. But as time goes by, the persistent soul becomes familiar and easy with the presence of God in all locales. Then the center of the soul wells up and fills the whole person with an awareness of God. The depths of God meet the abyss of solitude, and the soul knows no greater joy than the encounter with the Beloved One.

> Bless the LORD, my soul;
>> all my being, bless his holy name!
> Bless the LORD, my soul;
>> do not forget all the gifts of God.
>> PSALM 103:1-2

— 🌿 —

O Great God Who Dwells Within Me, I know that the depths of you far surpass the limits of my human frame. There is no way the fullness of your Being can be taken in my frail self. But I offer you the solitude of my interior, the silent space of emptiness within me, for your resting place. Please wash over me and fill me with your fullness.

II.
SANCTITY OF LIFE

Saints Were Absorbed

> "It was because the saints were absorbed in God that they were truly capable of seeing and appreciating created things and it was because they loved Him alone that they alone loved everybody."
>
> *New Seeds of Contemplation*, 23

One notion of sanctity that has been transmitted to us throughout the history of Christianity has been the equation of holiness with detachment from the world. Many classical writers address the relationship between these themes in a way that confuses us today. We are not comfortable with a sanctity that scorns created reality and removes itself from contact with the larger world and its influences.

Contemporary Christians who are actively engaged with the social realities of modern life may, however, forget the Origin of all that is created. Today it is easy to become absorbed in all sorts of false gods that are promoted by cultural beliefs and scientific perspectives. We may begin to depend on our human abilities and be culturally supported in the elevation of our own capacities to transcend our limitations.

We may also begin to see and appreciate things from the vantage point of how they can serve our own agendas. This is a very subtle attitude that is fostered and condoned by a consumer society. It is easy to legitimize the accumulation of goods in a culture that measures our value by external standards.

The saints had a dramatically different perspective on created things. While their appreciation of them may have appeared comparable to our own at times, the foundation underlying their regard for the world was significantly different. They were absorbed in the One who authored creation. They were wrapped up in the Giver first and foremost.

This absorption provided a detachment from all that was created yet, paradoxically, also allowed them to relish in radical simplicity the gifts of created reality. They saw a deeper reality that brought new regard for the creation without producing a subtle greed for goods. God was their ultimate good. Nothing else was necessary, but they treasured what was given as a sign of God's ultimate goodness.

In relationship with other people, the saints saw the goodness of God hidden within those they encountered. Loving God alone freed them to love more fully those whom God gave them. The vast capacity of God's love overflowed in their hearts, empowering them beyond their human abilities to love even the seemingly unlovable. This love was not their own nor was it to their credit. It flowed out of relationship with the Divine to whom they were deeply committed and engaged.

Few of us find such undistracted absorption in God in our lives. In many ways, it is a gift of God, offered where there is a willingness to receive it. How many of us want to receive it, though? The holiness of the saints is in their willingness to be absorbed by God at the cost of their human agenda in order to be used more fully by God to appreciate the world and love in a way that far exceeds the limitedness of human affection.

> O God, you are my God—
> for you I long!
> For you my body yearns;
> for you my soul thirsts,
> Like a land parched, lifeless,
> and without water.
> So I look to you in the sanctuary
> to see your power and glory.
> PSALM 63:2-3

— ❦ —

Beloved of My Heart, there are so many things that distract me from making you central in my life. I glimpse your desire for me, and I frequently run from your invitation. I desire the holiness that leads me into absorption with you and thus allows me to be an appreciative, loving sign of your presence in the world. Bring me into the simplicity I need to choose you first and foremost without counting the cost.

He Knows the Mercy of God

> "The eyes of the saint make all beauty holy and the hands of the saint consecrate everything they touch to the glory of God, and the saint is never offended by anything and judges no man's sins because he does not know sin. He knows the mercy of God."
>
> *New Seeds of Contemplation,* 24-25

A story is told of a great desert father of the third century who was called to judge another desert dweller on some misbehavior. He did not want to go, but his brother abbas prevailed upon him. To make his point, he took a large pot with a hole in it, filled it with water, and laboriously carried it over the desert miles, leaving a trail of water in his passage. When his fellow monks saw him burdened with his leaky load, they ran out to inquire why he was carrying such a faulty vessel. With sadness in his heart, he told them that his sins ran out behind him and yet this day he was called to judge another man. The judgment was called off.

The remarkable thing about these great saintly men and women is their humility. This humility stems from having themselves been witnesses to the great mercy of God in their own lives. They have felt the benevolence of a God who forgives, and they know that they cannot in any way judge another person's journey. They know that they can only walk upright because a God of compassion has shown mercy to them.

Mercy is shown in many ways. It is shown in forgiveness as the abba in the story expressed it. It is shown in a prodigal and lavish form in God's generous contributions to our sustenance. The eyes of the saint see the extravagance of God in the creation that provides us with all that we need for our survival. The saint relishes the tiny gift of a cup of tea or a portion of bread as much as a fine meal with wine and cake. All things bear the beauty of the Giver and are signs of the mercy of God.

Everything becomes sacred, therefore. The sinner becomes a potential vessel for the mercy of God as much as the saint. The mountain peak and the water's depths speak of the glory of God and the mercy that allows us to continue, even in our brokenness. Our "leakiness" even reminds us of a mercy that is beyond us but that we must emulate.

As we handle the world, whether through human hearts, through hard labor, or through healing hands, we show God's mercy to us in our conscious choice to touch the world with care. We transmit the tradition of mercy through our regard for that which is sacred, which through the saint's eyes is everything. We consecrate on one another, our planet, our worship, and our work with deliberate strokes of appreciation.

In our humility we show that we, too, are the beneficiaries of the mercy of God. We know the beauty of God's prodigality and we, too, have eyes to see. Our sins run out behind us so we will not judge.

So I will allure her;
> I will lead her into the desert
> and speak to her heart.

I will espouse you to me forever:
> I will espouse you in right and in justice,
> in love and in mercy;

I will espouse you in fidelity,
> and you shall know the Lord.
>> Hosea 2:16, 21-22

— ❦ —

Beloved One, I carry the weakness of my own being on my back. You know the heaviness of that which I carry as well as you know the burden of my neighbor's heaviness. Both of us share your mercy. Remind me when I want to judge, out of anger or frustration or hurt, that your mercy makes everything and everyone beautiful—including me in my anger and pain. Open me to the humility of my own frailty and fullness in you. I want to see the Beauty that consecrates all that is and all that will be.

It Takes Heroic Humility to Be Yourself

> "How do you expect to reach your own perfection by leading somebody else's life? His sanctity will never be yours; you must have the humility to work out your own salvation in a darkness where you are absolutely alone....And so it takes heroic humility to be yourself and to be nobody but the man, or the artist, that God intended you to be."
>
> *New Seeds of Contemplation,* 100

The one thing the world does not need is another Francis of Assisi. As a matter of fact, the world does not need another Benedict of Nursia or Teresa of Avila or Ignatius of Loyola. The world has already gained the benefits of the unique gifts each of these great saints gave. They have lived their lives fully and heroically, as no one else could have.

What we do need today are saints alive with the unique passion of their own lives. We need people who are openly struggling to live faith within the darkness of their own circumstances, making choices in the ambiguity, and continuing to seek God, even when they feel absolutely alone.

Each person's "perfection" has its own face. It is a sanctity marked with its own cell structure, genetic makeup, and situational background. It has its own passionate striving that takes unique form in the person's choices and foibles. It is a holiness that is fundamentally alone yet linked with all those faithful pilgrims from previous centuries who had no better corner on the market of sanctity than we do. They just tried to live their fidelity in relationship to God as best they could. They tried to honor the uniqueness of their own life with the heroic humility of being themselves.

We need more artists today whose characteristic style of being a person of God bears its own color and contour. We need more heroes and heroines who listen to the words of wisdom from the ancestors and then integrate them in a fresh new way in light of their own giftedness, as God intended. We don't need replicas of past days. We need new flesh and new blood to take up the artist's brush and begin to paint fresh designs.

A man coming out of retreat once said, "Holiness is not perfection or the arrival at some final goal of sanctity. Holiness of life is the willingness to struggle." Each of us has a brave new world to walk in. Each of us carries our own pride and shortcomings that block our creative energies in our artistic act of becoming who we can fully be. It takes heroic humility to pick up the pieces of our lives with all their complexity and walk and dream and strive to be our mysterious self in the Great Mystery.

But that is what sanctity is. Walking in our own shoes, limping and running, and being formed by the journey. Our "perfection" comes with each step and each choice to keep moving toward the face of God. It takes heroic humility to be who we are.

The Lord answer you in time of distress;
> the name of the God of Jacob defend you!
May God send you help from the temple,
> from Zion be your support.

May God...
> grant what is in your heart,
>> fulfill your every plan.

PSALM 20:2-5

— ❦ —

O Mysterious Artist, who uses my life to paint new color for the world, give me the courage to receive your unique gifts in my life. Be my sanctuary when I become afraid of becoming that full being that is uniquely your presence within me. Sustain me and help me walk gracefully in the true beauty you call forth from me. Give me the heroic humility to be as you would have me be.

III.
SEEDS OF IDENTITY

Planted in My Liberty

> "The seeds that are planted in my liberty at every moment, by God's will, are the seeds of my own identity, my own reality, my own happiness, and my own sanctity."
>
> *New Seeds of Contemplation,* 33

As a human being, I am a relatively free creature. I can choose to respond in a multitude of ways to the numerous "seeds" God is sending my way. Each choice that I make paves the way for future choices, both big and small. They shape my personality, my sense of who I am, my direction and preferences, and my own unique spirituality.

When I was a child, God flooded me with stimuli to foster a sense of wonder in my soul. If circumstances in life allowed me to be drawn into this wonder, I developed an appreciation for life. My capacity to be filled with awe formed and freed me to recognize an ultimate mysterious Presence in the world around me. This awe would serve me later in life when difficulties would seem overwhelming, and I would feel like losing heart. Somehow this wonder grounded me and gave me hope. I could maintain a relatively positive attitude of trust amidst the many trials, knowing I was not abandoned or alone. Awe and appreciation formed a foundation where faith, hope, and love could grow.

Perhaps, however, those around me did not encourage my appreciation of God's Mystery. Maybe they had never learned it themselves from their parents or they were too oppressed to help a child become sensitive to God's gifts. They may have not seen God's beauty within me as a little being of God and they may have hurt me, damaging my fundamental trust in the world as a safe place to grow up. I may have become suspicious, defensive, or aggressive to protect myself. My foundation, then, was a negative one of mistrust and anxiety.

Each of us in looking at the inner granary of seeds that compose our life will inevitably find some bad seed along with some good seed. What is essential for us is to recognize where the bad seed may be poisoning the good seed; where attitudes of mistrust may need to be reformed in order to let the fullness of appreciation flood our identities. We may find ourselves needing to make choices consciously to foster the development of appreciation, even though it feels like a difficult discipline. Appreciation serves as the basis for our true spiritual identity in relationship to God.

Appreciation or lack of appreciation influences the way I see my reality. It shapes my view of happiness and my identity. It also assists or hinders the gradual emergence of my sanctity. Without a capacity for wonder, I cannot be filled with an awareness of God. Without this awesome awareness, I cannot embrace my humility willingly. I will always want to defend myself instead of surrender myself. Through awe and appreciation, however, I can know a greater freedom and happiness in relationship to God. These are the seeds within me of God's hope, seeds that are planted in my liberty.

"A sower went out to sow. And as he sowed, some seed fell on the path, and birds came and ate it up. Some fell on rocky ground, where it had little soil. It sprang up at once because the soil was not deep, and when the sun rose it was scorched, and it withered for lack of roots. Some seed fell among thorns, and the thorns grew up and choked it. But some seed fell on rich soil, and produced fruit, a hundred or sixty or thirtyfold. Whoever has ears ought to hear."

MATTHEW 13:3-9

Sower of Seeds, sow your spirit of awe in my heart. Let me recognize the wonder of life that you give me and freely respond to all the opportunities you offer me to know you more deeply. Let the harvest of faith, hope, and love within my heart and within my acts be fullfold in honor of your generosity to me.

The Secret of My Full Identity Is Hidden

> "The secret of my full identity is hidden in Him. He alone can make me who I am, or rather who I will be when at last I fully begin to be. But unless I desire this identity and work to find it with Him and in Him, the work will never be done."
>
> *New Seeds of Contemplation,* 33

A grain of sand lies seemingly dormant in the tissues of a mollusk's flesh. It is hidden from light and air, from eyes that would want to examine its surroundings and possibly dislodge it from its private haven. But that is not the greater good. A greater beauty is being shaped.

Miraculously, the inner lining of the oyster's body forms a blanket over the minuscule particle and gradually deposits around it milky secretions, layer upon layer. Slowly, over the lifetime of the oyster, these iridescent layers harden in concentric circles around the grain of sand. The natural contribution of the oyster's body forms an exquisite jewel, unique in its shape. It is formed partially by the irritation of life and the consolation in that struggle. In the privacy of these hidden tissues a magnificent pearl is formed.

"The secret of my full identity is hidden in Him," Merton tells us. Like the grain of sand, my soul lies mysteriously hidden in its infancy in the reaches of God's goodness. God's miraculous grace slowly makes me who I am, who I am meant to be, a unique gem with delightful radiance. The contours of my soul are formed partly through the struggle of daily irritations and challenges. But when the mercy of God envelopes my life, I grow increasingly beautiful and full.

I will never know the full loveliness of my own soul. It is hidden in God but actively moving me toward a harmonious ascent to what is good and life-giving for me. Just as it would be deadly to pry open the oyster to examine the condition of the pearl within, so it would be damaging to prematurely expect the full beauty of my spirit to manifest itself without the contribution of time and maturity. Wisdom, like a pearl, needs a proper cultivation period. Sometimes it requires a lifetime.

What I can do is readily seek goodness, truth, and faith as a means to fostering the formation of the jewel within me. If I grow in my conscious awareness of God's movement in my life, leading me to greater beauty within the discomforts and pains of life, I can collaborate through my consent to God in the work going on in the hidden depths of my person. I must trust that a jewel is being formed, despite the hiddenness of its growth. The formation of a jewel such as this takes the time that God knows is best for it.

Daily choices help the polished pearl emerge. Each time I choose to refrain from gossip or choose to speak reverently to another person, I maximize the smooth reception and application of God's grace. Though it is hidden, a pearl of great price is in formation within me nestled in the heart of God.

> "...the kingdom of heaven is like a merchant searching for fine pearls. When he finds a pearl of great price, he goes and sells all that he has and buys it."
>
> MATTHEW 13:45-46

— 🌿 —

Great Heart of God, I want to be hidden in your heart, willing and ready to be shaped by each discomfort and delight. I want to become a pearl of great price that you desire to have in your kingdom, radiant and reflective of a heart that says yes to all that you offer. Here is my soul, a fragile grain of hope that asks for your mercy and care to fashion it into a pearl worthy of your gaze.

Thousands of Winged Seeds

> "Every moment and every event of every man's life on earth plants something in his soul. For just as the wind carries thousands of winged seeds, so each moment brings with it germs of spiritual vitality that come to rest imperceptibly in the minds and wills of men."
> *New Seeds of Contemplation,* 14

The revelation of God continues each second. We have come to accept the fact that the revelation of God is found primarily in our Scriptures and most fully in the life of Jesus Christ. For Christians, this is a foundational assumption. But lest we become too limited in our understanding of and openness to revelation, God continues to rain down upon us indicators of God's love and attentiveness to our human hungers. The lavishness of this "gifting" is far beyond what our senses can take in and consciously assimilate. The seeds may lie dormant for days or years before we notice them. In fact, we may never notice them.

It is staggering to consider how God even now is planting seeds of new vitality within us at every breath. It is overwhelming to ponder how every event bears new messages of truth and potential for our expanded consciousness. These "winged seeds" are gifts to raise our awareness of God's benevolent presence in our lives. But they are so numerous that we cannot take them all in. It is as if we wear a filter that screens what we can absorb and blocks the rest.

The contemplative journey of prayer and reflection increases our capacity of awareness. Through a regular rhythm of deliberate interior quiet, we begin to ask questions about God's revelation to us in our daily lives. We may start to ask ourselves, "What is the kernel of truth in this event? What challenge is being offered to me by God through this person's criticism, compliments, or insights?" We may find ourselves more detached from our own willful control over our lives and more willing to receive the surprises that God wants to reveal to us.

If we were consciously and conscientiously trying to absorb and integrate the multitudes of God's messages to us each day, we may feel exhausted with the process. That may be partly because we try to grab God's gifts and hold on to them in our hunger to understand, to grow, and to perfect ourselves. In fact, God is lavish in these gifts. They overwhelm us because in some way we are still trying to control the process. In a way, we are greedy for God's gifts, wanting to get all we can.

God, however, is showering them upon us with each beat of our heart. If we can relax with this immeasurable generosity, we can receive the gifts in a detached way and not cling to them. The providence of God is consistent, though diverse, in its forms. Just as the Israelites had to learn that the manna in the desert would be there as long as they needed it and there was no need to greedily stockpile it for the next day, so God's daily gifts of insight, patience, and spiritual nourishment will be there according to our needs and according to God's design for our lives.

> "Do not be amazed that I told you, 'You must be born from above.' The wind blows where it wills, and you can hear the sound it makes, but you do not know where it comes from or where it goes; so it is with everyone who is born of the Spirit."
>
> JOHN 3:7-8

Prodigal God, *you shower me with life-sustaining gifts so numerous that I cannot take them in. I want to see more clearly the clues you have for me in living my life to the fullest. Keep me from becoming greedy with your gifts or controlling in my own life's direction. Help me to receive gracefully the seeds of truth you offer and trust the growth you will bring forth in me through awareness.*

IV.
INTEGRATION

Body and Soul as One

> "If the two are separated from one another, there is no longer a person, there is no longer a living subsisting reality made in the image and likeness of God. The 'marriage' of body and soul in one person is one of the things that makes man the image of God; and what God has joined, no man can separate without danger to his sanity."
>
> *New Seeds of Contemplation*, 27

As a human being, I have a soul. It is what makes me distinct from other living creatures on the planet. I have a spiritual nature with a desire to reach out to the mystery of God. I have a nature that cares about my world and others within it.

That spiritual nature is housed in a body unique to me. Without this body, I could not connect with the world as it is created. The body is my bridge for contact with other people, with the earth, and with the universe. Through my embodiment, I can touch other people physically. I can give expression to the passion of God within me through song, dance, and words; and my emotions have a vehicle in my limbs and nerves through which to communicate the movements of my inner life.

If I were just a spirit, I would have no concrete way to tell the world about my existence and thoughts. Many philosophers and spiritualists through the ages have tried to downplay the importance of my body for spiritual life. They have not acknowledged the necessity of their bodies for recording their ideas about the spiritual journey. They have been confused and afraid of the impulses and abuses of people whose embodiment led them into conflict. Fear of poor choices made them deny their bodies as if they were the sources of the evil they perceived.

But how could I feel joy without a beating heart, without eyes through which to see the world and a brain through which I could decipher the message? How could I communicate this wonder in my soul without a tongue to speak it and others to hear it through their enfleshed being?

The body needs my spirit to help it channel its energies toward healthy expressions. The spirit needs my body to express itself into the world so that it can live a communal life in communication with other people. Thomas Merton says, "If the two are separated from one another, there is no longer a person...made in the image and likeness of God." It is this "marriage" that makes us human in God's image, capable of transcending through our spirit and able to express that relationship through our bodies.

We are called into harmonious living within the various dimensions of our humanity. We are asked to recognize all the gifts of our humanness—body, soul, and mind. There is a constant dialogue of communication going on inside each of us as we see, reflect, and make meaning out of the world God has given us. Without proper respect and appreciation for all aspects of our humanness, we run the risk of betraying and debasing the image of God within us.

> You formed my inmost being;
> > you knit me in my mother's womb.
> I praise you, so wonderfully you made me;
> > wonderful are your works!
> My very self you knew;
> > my bones were not hidden from you,
> When I was being made in secret,
> > fashioned as in the depths of the earth.
> > > PSALM 139:13-15

— ❦ —

Beloved Creator, my body confuses me at times with all its needs and drives. But I know deep inside, this drive is for your honor and glory so that I may seek you with my whole being. Thank you for the limbs, the eyes, the tongue, and the words through which I can reach out to you in the world and touch what you've created. Let your Spirit guide me in my expressions of love and bring me into harmony within myself and with you.

Integrate the Unknown and the Known

> "The function of faith is not to reduce mystery to rational clarity, but to integrate the unknown and the known together in a living whole, in which we are more and more able to transcend the limitations of our external self."
>
> *New Seeds of Contemplation,* 136

We live in a highly rational era. The birth of science has pushed us to emphasize reason and observability as important methods for determining what is factual. There is a strong emphasis on proving things in order to validate our belief in them. Factual information becomes a key element in defining what we put our faith in. We don't really like risking our security on unknowns.

But there are many ways to know. We know through scientific research and the knowledge of logic. Unquestionably, this knowledge is elevated by our culture. We also know through intuition and the knowledge of the heart. Our sixth sense often guides us in making important decisions that cannot be made through logic alone.

In addition to these "knowns," there are many unknowns that we will never truly understand. We are finite beings in our consciousness. We can only see part of the picture; we can never comprehend the complete whole. The limits of our senses and mental capacities hold us bound to a certain degree.

But our capacity to transcend or move beyond these limitations is what makes us remarkable as human beings. We can know rationally, but we can also move beyond rational and intuitive knowledge to wisdom.

Wisdom is "a knowing," integrating what we can know rationally with that which we know intuitively. It does not stop there, however. Wisdom also demands a respect for that which cannot be known. It involves maintaining a reverence for the mystery that is beyond us, equally real but escaping calculation and definability. Through wisdom, we glimpse a new horizon from which to perceive our world. We find a new appreciation for what we cannot know as well as for what we think we understand.

Wisdom allows us to retain a certain humility before all that we know. Faith is born in a humility that recognizes the bit of mystery even in the known. That which is known in seeming clarity is never fully understood as the divine One sees it. Faith allows God to be God in that fullness and remembers that humanity's limits should lead us back into reverence for this fullness.

It is through this faith that we transcend the boundaries of our human mind and know a wider perspective not based on mental gymnastics, logic, or precision. In reverence for the mystery our hearts expand, acknowledging the wisdom that surpasses all understanding. In faith we integrate the known with the unknown in surrender to this mystery. We accept the lack of clarity and know that there is a beauty in "the cloud of unknowing."

> My soul rests in God alone,
>   from whom comes my salvation.
> God alone is my rock and salvation,
>   my secure height; I shall never fall.
>   PSALM 62:2-3

— ❦ —

O Great Mystery of the Universe, my mind and my heart clamor to know more fully the wonders that you have created in the world. But more deeply, my soul yearns for peace with that which I cannot know but wish I could. Let the wisdom of faith you offer me be enough for my thirsting and often greedy mind. Let me peacefully enter the cloud that embraces you and find it humbly comfortable and yet alluring, drawing me into greater willingness and faith.

The World I Am Part Of

> "The world as pure object is something that is not there. It is not a reality outside us for which we exist....It is a living and self-creating mystery of which I am myself a part, of which I am myself, my own unique door. When I find the world in my own ground, it is impossible for me to be alienated by it."
>
> *Contemplation in a World of Action*, 154-155

As human beings, we care about our world. We care about the health of the planet, the future for our children, and the current affairs of the day. Human beings are the only species whose concern for their world makes them want to shape it and reform it if it is going awry. We consciously and actively play a part in the formation of history and the survival of the planet.

How can we divorce ourselves from the living environment that sustains our existence? The only way we could ignore the intimate connection between ourselves and the ecosphere is to objectify it and see it for our use only. Many generations of people have maintained this attitude. They have seen themselves and the world as two separate entities with little interdependence.

This remote "pure object" of the world does not exist. There is no reality separate from ourselves, Merton reminds us. The world is given shape through human input, and the human species is formed by the world's changes. We cannot distance ourselves from our world, for we cannot exist without it.

At the same time, we have a distinct role in fostering the relationship of harmony on the planet. Each of us enters the world individually through our own unique door, our unrepeatable set of circumstances, genetic combinations, and special capacities. We look at and appreciate our world through the lenses of our history, our physical makeup, our families of origin, and our technical abilities. The world has already impacted us by the time we are old enough to reflect on it. It is within our experience and our survival as human beings.

Standing on the ground of history, standing on the earth that many have trod before, this planet which has sustained whole tribes with its air, land, and water, we can feel ourselves a part of this world. We can know a deeper relationship that overrides the alienation that an industrializing society produces.

The world is partly of my construction. I have given it form through my life, and it has impacted and shaped me as well. This is a living, self-creating mystery of which I myself am a part, capable, responsible, and caring. I am a cocreator of history. I am a midwife for the birth of the next generation of caregivers who will shape the world after me.

In Chinese art, unlike Western, the human person rarely commands a central spot. Rather, the human person is off to the side, participating in the flow of the scene without dominating it. We co-create in interdependence. God is central. The world is in us because the

Creator has linked us together. Blessed be the name of the Lord.

> Streams of the river gladden the city of God,
>   the holy dwelling of the Most High.
> God is in its midst; it shall not be shaken.
>
> PSALM 46:5-6A

— ❦ —

Creator of the World, teach me to respect the world that you have given us and to recognize how I shape it through my own attitudes and actions. I tend to see the world as separate from myself and take control of it. Yet I know you are the center of all creation, and I need the reminder that the stream is as sacred as my own bloodstream; the breeze is as precious as my own breath.

V.
THE GOD WITHIN

God Shines Back
Into His Own House

> "Love comes out of God and gathers us to God in order to pour itself back into God through all of us and bring us all back to Him on the tide of His own infinite mercy. So we all become doors and windows through which God shines back into His own house."
>
> *New Seeds of Contemplation,* 67

Like the surging tide of the ocean, perpetual, powerful, and magnetic, God's love pulls us into God's self.

There is an alluring quality to this presence that is both deep within us yet that extends far beyond the parameters of our bodies and consciousness. We belong to a God who exceeds our wildest imagination.

God is Love. All our preconceived ideas about what Love is like pale next to this reality. Thomas Merton reminds us that the love that is poured out upon us from God does not return to God empty. There is a spiraling increase in God's generosity to us. More love comes forth from God's love.

Imagine that infinite wave, the divine Mystery that topples us by overwhelming our senses, our imagination, our hopes, and our memories with Divine fullness. Many mystics and contemplatives speak of God's intoxicating attraction. God comes out of God's Self and draws us in through love. As we are filled with that grace, God returns us to our world awakened and willing to share that love.

The divine Mystery is infinite yet so compassionate that God willingly pours God's Self into human vessels with clay feet and wobbly knees. However feeble, we become the icons of God's living presence in the world. We become "the doors and windows" through which God reveals love to the world. Like a radiant light, God shines from our eyes, our words, and our acts.

It is a merciful God who surges, swells, and subsides in us. This mercy calls forth from us a concrete image of concern for the world. Our vitality, our mind, our transcendent capacity, and our culture can reflect a Creator God in compassionate form. How can we go about "shining" God's light into the house of the world? How do we shine back into the house of God, the Church? Finally, how do we keep our own light burning brightly so that our inner temple does not fall into darkness?

Love begets love. Like a wave, the love of an individual can evoke compassion in another. The active display of concern warms the many hearts who witness it. The love spreads for many to see. Compassion then generates community. Others are brought into the swirling dynamic of God's revelation of care. The witness to love can inspire others to carry the tide of concern further.

We are like fragments of shells scattered on a beach. We are picked up by the wave that promises new crests and are compelled through love to reach new peaks.

Then, smoothly polished by the wave, we are invited to share that beauty with those who pass by us. We are signs of God's active involvement in our world. In the spiral of relationship with God, we are gradually transformed in intimacy and mercy each day. Let us catch the wave.

> Here deep calls to deep in the roar of
>   your torrents.
> All your waves and breakers sweep
>   over me.
>
> PSALM 42:8

— 🌿 —

Shining Light of My Soul, I welcome your embrace, your call, your invitation to dance in the new light that is your presence alive within me. I desire for my house to be filled with your mercy, that I might become a shining sign of you, filling the earth with hope and joy. Carry me in your wave, Beloved One, and lead me to your house.

Christ Will Be Able to Love

> "My true personality will be fulfilled in the Mystical Christ in this one way above all, that through me, Christ and His Spirit will be able to love you and all men and God the Father in a way that would be possible in no one else."
> *New Seeds of Contemplation*, 67

There is so much talk today about "fulfillment." Everyone seems to be looking for it. We judge the happiness of our lives often on whether or not we feel "fulfilled."

There is legitimacy in some of that search. If we seek part of our fulfillment in contributing to the world by making it a better place, we can see that this desire serves a larger purpose than merely individual needs for success. Each of us has a fundamental striving to see the work of our hands as valuable and valued. There is something fulfilling about this.

This statement of Thomas Merton, however, suggests that fulfillment of one's personality is linked to the Mystical Body of Christ. There is a unique role each of us plays in bringing love into the world in a new way. Merton says that our true personality will be realized only if we embrace our unique role within the Mystical Body of Christ and live that love actively.

Our limited human love cannot possibly reach this fulfillment of its own volition or by its own effort.

Strangely, our fulfillment involves our surrender to a greater love that is beyond us, the love of Christ and his Spirit. We willingly become conduits for the flow of divine love. We assent to let the Spirit of Christ use our uniqueness to reveal love to all people, including ourselves. Without our consent, the full expression of Christ's love would be hampered.

Equally significant is the unique way Christ's love for God is revealed through us. No one else can express love for God in the exact way that Christ will express it through me. Without my deliberate assent, something will be missing in the fullness of human devotion to the Mystery of God. Complementing this, my human witness testifies to the greatness of God so that others may know its importance in my life. My authentic dedication to the God of Jesus Christ can impact a different circle of people than anyone else's.

All of this may sound confusing. It is not easy for us to see our fulfillment achieved in and through another Person, Jesus Christ. It seems paradoxical that we can shine best by letting another shine through us. That is part of the mystery of being in relationship with God in the Christian tradition.

We are invited to embrace our uniqueness and offer it to Christ to be used for the greater good of building up the Body of Christ. We are called to willingly allow the Spirit of love to radiate from our beings to the unique circle of those to whom we are called to witness. In that embrace and in that surrender, our fulfillment will surprisingly be realized. I will be filled full with a Presence that is not exclusive to me but who distinctively uses my personality for a divine intention: to show the love of God.

> I urge you therefore, brothers [and sisters], by the mercies of God, to offer your bodies as a living sacrifice, holy and pleasing to God, your spiritual worship. Do not conform yourself to this age but be transformed by the renewal of your mind, that you may discern what is the will of God, what is good and pleasing and perfect.
>
> ROMANS 12:1-2

— 🌿 —

Father of Christ, I want to be full of your Spirit, radiating what is your love for the world through all the gifts that you give me. Give me the courage to surrender my ideas of fulfillment. Teach me your ways, O Lord, and grant me the freedom to let my life be a witness to your greatness.

Each One Is Christ

> "The unity of the members of Christ is such that together they form one Person, one Christ, and yet each one personally 'is Christ.'"
> *Disputed Questions,* 104

Look at the back of your hand. See the tiny geometric shapes of the cells that make up your skin. They are all unique. Even within the millions that make up one person's skin, science tells us, no two are alike nor are they like the cells in anyone else's body.

We, as Christians, live in the Body of Christ. We can look at this in two different ways. First of all, on the personal level we are called to be a cell of Christ in a unique way according to our gifts, characteristics, and personality traits. Each fiber of our bodies, each action, each attitude we reflect, must remind people of the presence of Christ within the world and raise their awareness of God. A particular form of Christ's presence will be specific for each one of us as unique as a cell in the human body. Christ will shine forth from each within the uniqueness that God has created in us. Therefore, in a personal way Christ lives within your cellular structure—within your unique personhood. You are called to be Christ in the world within this.

You are also called to recognize the uniqueness of Christ within other persons you meet. This recognition appears to be easier with some people than with others.

Some people appear to be more attractive and appealing in their humanness than others. Yet just as you are a particular cell of Christ to the world through your unique gifts, the checker in the grocery store is also a unique image of God, keeping alive the Body of Christ in his or her own fashion. We can view another "cell" through different eyes with a new appreciation when we recognize that God's presence in the world is being revealed in a special way in this person.

Here is where the second aspect of living in the Body of Christ comes into play. What is unique to Christianity is the call to unity as members within the Body of Christ. Individually, we are personal witnesses of Christ, but we are also called as a community to witness to the unity of the Body of Christ. Each of us, like cells in the Mystical Body, forms the skeleton and muscles that make Christ visible today. We help it as a whole to move toward health or away from it. We are united in relationship as sinews bound together through the Spirit of love.

At some point in this relationship, we begin to see ourselves in relationship with others in a new way. If we are ill, the whole Body is affected. If another is hungry, the Body is impaired. Some universal connection ties me in my humanity to my neighbors. Their struggles become my struggles. I become my neighbor in a new awareness of solidarity, intimacy, and compassion. I cannot judge or criticize them without becoming aware of my own acts of weakness, brokenness, or arrogance.

Thus, I am Christ. The washerwoman is Christ. Judas is Christ. In such humility, I am also the washerwoman. I am also Judas. Just as I am involved with the Person of

Christ in contemplation, I am involved with the Person of Christ on the streets, sharing in the love offered each person in him and in every betrayal of him. Out of the nakedness of humility, compassion is born. In this compassion, community in the Person of Christ can be born as well. Compassion and community depend on each other. In the Person of Christ, all that was divided is brought together and a new identity forms in a union of diversities.

> For in him all the fullness was pleased to dwell,
>   and through him to reconcile all things for
>   him,
>   making peace by the blood of his cross
>   [through him], whether those on earth
>   or those in heaven.
>
> COLOSSIANS 1:19-20

Reconciler God, I see your face in this mirror image before me with unique cells, eyes, and skin. This reflection is me but more profoundly you. Another mirror presents itself to me in the person on the street who begs for dignity when dignity seems lacking. Remove the callouses from my eyes that I may see your eyes, especially in the unappealing, the alarming, and the confusing. Give me fresh vision and a clean heart to reach to your Person where I would rather not extend my hand.

VI.
LABOR

To Do the Work Carefully

> "To do the work carefully and well, with love and respect for the nature of my task and with due attention to its purpose, is to unite myself to God's will in my work. I become His instrument. He works through me."
>
> *New Seeds of Contemplation,* 19

The experience of creativity is a share in God's creative image within us. When we work, we shape our world, giving it a touch of our uniqueness. We contribute to the upbuilding of society.

Our work gives us a concrete place to express our creative ability. Just as God took delight in the creation of Adam, so we take delight in a job well done. It is an essential part of our humanness to put our hands to work in order to produce something of value.

Thomas Merton tells us that to "do the work carefully and well, with love and respect" unites us to the purposes of God. To approach our tasks with a reverent disposition implies that we approach our world differently from the way many tend to do in the modern world. We are jostled about in elevators, competed with at busy intersections, and threatened with deadlines. It is a difficult milieu to approach with love and respect.

How can we become God's instrument and let God work through us in such a fast-paced, seemingly hostile work environment? How can we keep alive the intention to unite ourselves to the will of God in our work?

The challenge is to find simple ways to regenerate our awareness of God's presence in the everyday movements of our lives. We can introduce a gentle spirit into the work environment as well as into our approach to ourselves and our colleagues. Sometimes the smallest gestures can foster that love and respect. Perhaps it will be in a deliberate choice to handle the material world reverently by not slamming doors and file cabinets, to handle the world gently instead. In this choice, we modify little actions that draw us into a communion of care with God as our guide.

With ourselves and others, that gentleness can be fostered with inquiries of concern, silent prayers of petition, and statements of appreciation. A gruff salesclerk frequently will soften when a concerned stranger inquires if she's having a hard day. A word of support to a coworker can ease isolation and bond two workers in the task at hand. Where words or gestures are not possible, an intercessory prayer for the well-being of the other consciously brings the mystery of God into the petitioner's mind and heart. Even a meditative attentiveness to dusting the furniture can be like a caress for the world.

We become God's instrument each in our own way. In each place we go and in the work we perform lies an opportunity for our collaboration with the Spirit. God works through our work and our activities. We cocreate with God in shaping a world that can be one of greater gentleness and compassion if we "do the work carefully and well, with love and respect."

...the law of the LORD is their joy;
>   God's law they study day and night.
> They are like a tree
>   planted near streams of water,
>   that yields its fruit in season;
> Its leaves never wither;
>   whatever they do prospers.
>
> PSALM 1:2-3

— ❦ —

Creative God, my work is your work. My yield is your yield. All that I do, all that I gain, is yours. I delight in the gifts you give me, the work of my hands, the thoughts of my mind, the words of my mouth. Let every action of mine today give you honor and glory. Let every gesture, every interaction, every accomplishment, be done in reverence and in an awareness that you are my source of strength. Blessed be the fruit of your handiwork through me today.

Make All Activity Bear Fruit

> "No matter how little you may have learned of God in prayer, compare your acts with that little; order them by that measure. Try to make all activity bear fruit in the same emptiness and silence and detachment you have found in contemplation."
>
> *New Seeds of Contemplation,* 192

How do you open doors? Do you assert yourself against them and kick them when you get frustrated? When you are on your way out, do you slam them shut? Do you ever think of how you handle the door?

We have all jerked doors open and slammed them shut. But in some way, our handling of doors is indicative of the way we handle the world. The way we touch our world is reflected in the littlest of gestures. Each activity reflects a reverent or irreverent regard for creation and our approach to living in it.

In contemplation, in peak moments when the harmony of God's benevolence is glimpsed, we surrender our control, our hostility, and our insistence on rushing through life to our next destination. We slow down and sense a new respect for ourselves, generated by a felt experience of God's regard for us. It is natural, fluid, and easy.

However we experience God in prayer, we are to

order our life accordingly. Even the smallest gesture can be reordered to reflect and sustain the reverence in relationship to the Creator. The way I touch my world can remind me of the way God touches me and calls me to caress the world from within that relationship. Every action, every step, every thought, is thus gradually transformed through a conscious decision to live gently according to what I have found in contemplation.

Native American, Buddhist, and Eastern Christian contemplative traditions advocate raising our awareness of the attitudes behind the smallest of gestures by looking at how we perform them. Ignatius of Loyola counseled people to examine their actions twice daily to help them refine their awareness of how they were living in relationship to God.

In many ways, such a reflective awareness is an invitation to grow in courtesy. Our divine, courteous God has given us all that we need. In respect, we courteously touch God through the tangible ways we touch our world. We can foster a consciousness that is more alert to God's presence in the world by choosing to "make all activity bear fruit." We empty ourselves of our own arrogance and noise by slowing down our pace, focusing our attention on the handling of our world, and choosing courteously to reorder our activity in line with our reverence for God.

Everyday life is the seedbed for greater choices. It is the door through which we practice what we preach and incarnate in minute ways what we hope to be able to do when larger challenges present themselves. We can refine our attitudes through the daily practice of reverence. The door is open. How would you like to handle it?

> Lord, my heart is not proud;
>   nor are my eyes haughty.
> I do not busy myself with great matters,
>   with things too sublime for me.
> Rather, I have stilled my soul,
>   hushed it like a weaned child.
> Like a weaned child on its mother's lap,
>   so is my soul within me.
> ...hope in the Lord,
>   now and forever.
>
> Psalm 131

— 🌿 —

Reverent Creator, you touch my heart with the tenderness of a mother with her child. You courteously invite me to intimacy with you, trusting in your mercy, responding to your generosity to me. Transform my attitudes as you shape my actions according to your way. Let me walk this Earth with reverence, touching it as I would want to touch you. Let me become a gentle icon of your presence in the world.

Society Without Wisdom

> "Science and technology are indeed admirable in many respects; and if they fulfill their promises, they can do much for man. But they can never solve his deepest problems. On the contrary, without wisdom, with the intuition and freedom that enable man to return to the root of his being, science can only precipitate him still further into the centrifugal flight that flings him, in all his compact and uncomprehending isolation, into the darkness of outer space without purpose and without objective."
>
> *Faith and Violence,* 224

Almost all people in North America and Western Europe know the merits of industrialization. Physically and functionally, life seems more comfortable and leisure more readily available as a result of it. Our refrigeration is relatively consistent and our telephones amazingly dependable. Therefore, our vaccines and our food are kept safe from contamination, and our communication is easily facilitated technologically. The predictability of electricity fuels the safe usage of computers, fax equipment, and answering machines in the business world. Satellite systems assist the transmission of information, bringing us within moments to the scene of catastrophes and news events.

However, technology is a mixed blessing. Insidiously, it also can deter the spiritual growth that is humanity's most distinctive heritage. The values of efficiency, quantity, and speed behind technological advancement can derail the process of full humanization by focusing us on merely functional accomplishments and success. This focus can flatten the spiritual capacities that distinguish us as human. It can alienate us from the Source of our creative power and from one another.

Our technology is a result of the creative use of human reason. The human hunger to know has given birth to science. But science looks at parts and how they are composed, often forgetting to see the whole and how the parts fit together. Sometimes we forget to note the effects that this "partial view" can have on us. Science and technology can fragment our sense of relationship with self and with others.

The informational "knowledge" of science must be paired with the intuitive "knowing" that comes with wisdom. The information of modern science must be integrated with the revelation of the ages and personally assimilated. Wisdom cannot be quantified, analytically determined, or technologically manufactured. It comes from a gracious melding of personal insight and the great spiritual traditions of the ages. This allows us to root ourselves spiritually in the midst of tremendous change in an industrializing culture.

Science and technology can never solve our deeper problems. Wisdom, however, reconnects us on a deeper level to the spiritual dimension of life. To see the whole picture requires intuition and imagination as well as reason. Within this wisdom, we can exercise a healthy freedom that leads us more deeply into our humanity and our relatedness to the Divine. Wisdom can heal our alienation and bring us into right relationship with our Creator.

> The earth is the LORD's and all it holds,
>   the world and those who live there.
> For God founded it on the seas,
>   established it over the rivers.
> Who can go up the mountain of the LORD?
>   Who can stand in his holy place?
> "The clean of hand and pure of heart...."
>
> PSALM 24:1-4

— 🌿 —

Mystery of God, Vast and Rare, the great works of our own hands are nothing compared to those of yours, nor could they have come to be without your gracious creative power within us. In humility we ask you to remind us of our role in creating with you a world that is just and merciful. Help us to not let greed, speed, and pride disintegrate our awareness of our relationship with you and that which is created. Let our works be bright mirrors of your creative power and faithfully reflect a respect for the planet you have given us.

VII.
SOLIDARITY AND SERVICE

A Body of Broken Bones

> "As long as we are on earth, the love that unites us will bring us suffering by our very contact with one another, because this love is the resetting of a Body of broken bones."
>
> *New Seeds of Contemplation,* 72

By virtue of being human, I am vulnerable to you because part of being human is caring. Human beings are unique in their fundamental concern for the world and their being in it. That vulnerability opens me up to others and their experiences too. By my very contact with another, I am risking the discovery of my ability to suffer. I experience the pathos of being connected with a larger reality beyond the parameters of my skin.

The love Christ spoke of addresses this capacity. Christ builds on this fundamental way of being in human beings and takes it further. He elevates this vulnerability by embracing it in his own humanness, in his own body. Once we sense what it is to be part of the Body of Christ, a larger reality of connectedness that transcends historical boundaries and geographical distances, we know within us a whole new level of sensitivity and responsibility.

There are times when we would rather not cross the threshold into that new level of existence. There is greater pain involved than there was in our former sleepy awareness. It is not always pleasant, simple, or neat. We may have to get involved on a level that threatens the comfortable assumptions we made before. But despite the discomfort, to go back would be to ignore the Body that we know we are part of.

Instead, we stand before the broken limbs of poverty, injustice, hatred, and inequality. We see the scars of such wounds in our own churches, in our society, and in our homes. We may feel cowardly in facing the magnitude of this suffering.

But we are a Body of broken bones. Our human love, though insufficient without the Holy Spirit, can be used by divine creativity and healing to make straight the crippled limbs of the many broken bodies we see. We cannot do it ourselves. Our efforts will always be marred by the shortsightedness and selfishness of our own perspectives and wounds. But our desire can be consecrated and the Spirit of God freed through us to comfort and strengthen weary hands and hearts.

Because we love, we will be vulnerable. Because we seek God, we will be empowered within that vulnerability to stand within the healing process and let love reset the bones. Rubbing shoulders with one another will reveal our shadow sides, but the light of the mystery of God can still unite us within our willingness.

We are the beings who care, made in the image and likeness of the great Care-Being. Our foibles and feebleness compose the Body of Christ as much as our successes and strengths. We embrace and surrender both, knowing that love writes straight with crooked lines and skeletons are made strong with healing touches.

Strengthen the hands that are feeble,
>> make firm the knees that are weak,
Say to those whose hearts are frightened:
>> Be strong, fear not!
Here is your God,
>> he comes with vindication;
With divine recompense
>> he comes to save you.
Then will the eyes of the blind be opened,
>> the ears of the deaf be cleared.

>> Isaiah 35:3-5

Great Being of Care, I see my brokenness before me, and I am horrified. I turn to my neighbor and see it there too. The Body is twisted by narrowness and fear. Heal that which you can use in our brokenness to make the Body strong. Let me not be afraid to suffer the touch of care by embracing another's harshness and letting my body, my spirit, my heart, be used in the resetting of the Body of broken bones.

Share Some of Their Poverty

> "It is easy enough to tell the poor to accept their poverty as God's will when you yourself have warm clothes and plenty of food and medical care and a roof over your head and no worry about the rent. But if you want them to believe you—try to share some of their poverty and see if you can accept it as God's will yourself!
>
> *New Seeds of Contemplation,* 179

For people living in the developed world where goods are relatively available and shelter reasonably accessible, it is often a touchy subject to bring up the reality of poverty. It is not a comfortable subject in our secure world if it directly challenges our established norms and standard of living. Interestingly enough, the standard of a modest lifestyle has dramatically shifted with industrialization and technological advances. What used to be assumed as a luxury is now viewed as a necessity. Hence, every newlywed couple assumes the need for a microwave oven or an answering machine as a part of basic survival in the Northern Hemisphere.

Such concerns, when measured against the larger norm of the two thirds of the world's population living outside this culture, seem irrelevant. Many of the "needs" we are accustomed to today are viewed as "luxuries" elsewhere. We have begun to confuse "wants" with "needs." Some would take it so far as to say our "greeds" have replaced our "needs."

Thomas Merton challenges our complacence. No one finds poverty easy, appealing, or redemptive when it is imposed on one by structures and systems that dehumanize people. Simplicity of life when freely chosen can bring people to greater awareness of their dependence on God, but that is not to be equated with impoverishment.

So how are we "who have" meant to deal with the magnitude of the needs of a world of "have nots"? Merton's response is radical but freeing: "If you have money, consider that perhaps the only reason God allowed it to fall into your hands was in order that you might find joy and perfection in giving it all away" (*New Seeds of Contemplation*, 179).

Think of the delightful prodigality of living a life where one is constantly seeking ways and means of showering others with the gains of one's own life. Viewed from a certain perspective, it's clownish and playful. Rather than being an obligation based on duty, it becomes an opportunity for surprise and creativity. It reshapes the entire concept of stewardship into an experience of collaboration with the Divine of making others healthy and happy.

Few of us have great resources to utilize to make significant monetary changes in world economics. The mystery of God is not asking for this from those with modest incomes. However, we all share in the poverty of life. We can use that which is given to us to encourage and lighten the load of poverty in the world around us. We can assume the role of creative collaborator with God in seeking out small and large ways to spread the goods around. In "giving it all away," we find greater joy and perfection of heart that leads us to the real treasure in the lap of the Lord.

> This, rather, is the fasting that I wish:
>   releasing those bound unjustly,
>   untying the thongs of the yoke;
> Setting free the oppressed,
>   breaking every yoke;
> Sharing your bread with the hungry,
>   sheltering the oppressed and the homeless;
> Clothing the naked when you see them,
>   and not turning your back on your own.
>   ISAIAH 58:6-7

True Treasure of My Heart, these words are hard for me to hear sometimes. My spirit may be willing, but it is difficult to let go of the goods of this world that also give me some satisfaction. Help me to find the real treasure of sharing my time, my energy, and my resources more completely with those who present themselves to me in need, whether those whom I know and see often or those at a distance. Give me a taste of that radical freedom of spirit that will help me increasingly to see and respond creatively to those I can offer myself to.

Hell Is Nothing in Common

> "Hell is where no one has anything in common with anybody else except the fact that they all hate one another and cannot get away from one another and from themselves."
>
> *New Seeds of Contemplation,* 123

A story is told of a man who died and arrived at heaven's gate. His guardian angel met him to give him a tour of the place. "I'm going to show you a bit of hell before we proceed further," the angel said as they walked into a large banquet hall. In the center of the room was a huge table loaded with food. Surrounding the table were emaciated, groaning figures of human beings, sunk down in their chairs. The man inquired why these people were so starved with so much food in front of them. The angel pointed to three-foot-long forks, which he indicated were the only restriction placed on these inhabitants of hell. "They must use these forks to eat." The forks were far too long to turn and insert in their own mouths.

The angel proceeded on to the next room, in which were an equally bountiful table and equally long forks. The people here were fat and laughing, satisfied with plenty of food and camaraderie. "The same restrictions apply here in Heaven," the angel pointed out, "But here people have learned to solve the problem by feeding one another and allowing themselves to be fed by their neighbor."

To be sent to a place where people only thought of themselves, where competition and greed were the main approach to life, and where one felt basically alone and lonely would be a hellish experience. Not to feel affinity with others because one's life choices make relationship difficult is a *living* hell.

Isolation from others and exaltation of one's self are two ways that we insulate ourselves from the responsibilities involved in being connected with others. They are two excuses we often use unconsciously to protect ourselves from the demands of being in relationship with others. We shield ourselves from the challenges others might make to our lifestyle, to our attitudes, even to our understanding of Church because we really don't want to enter in and risk intimacy or change.

Hell is a place with few changes. People refusing to see the commonality between human and human, regardless of their socioeconomic status or state of health, introduce a foretaste of hell into their lives. They cannot wait to seclude themselves behind the barriers of prejudice, fear, or superiority. It's safer there. They will not be required to look a second time at the long-term starvation of their heart in its disconnection with a larger body of humanity.

The obvious walls are easy to spot. Some have guard dogs and security police. The more common ones that disconnect us are the hidden ones that we construct inside ourselves to keep the needs of others out of sight. We build inside of ourselves a hellish community of one. To find heaven and to feed ourselves we have to be able to look across the table and extend a hand of solidarity so that others might live.

You have been told....what is good,
    and what the LORD requires of you:
Only to do the right and to love goodness,
    and to walk humbly with your God.
                                MICAH 6:8

— 🌿 —

Generous God, you have given us all that we need to sustain ourselves. You have stretched out your hand over eons of time and space to touch our lives and teach us how to touch one another. I still get scared by the AIDS victim and the homeless man and woman on the street. I still feel awkward when the hungry child tugs at my sleeve for food. Show me how to get my hands out of my pockets and extend them to those whose needs reflect my own.

Solidarity and Service 🌿 81

And Now I Owe

> "And now I owe everyone else in the world a share in that life. My first duty is to start, for the first time, to live as a member of a human race which is no more (and no less) ridiculous than I am myself. And my first human act is the recognition of how much I owe everybody else."
>
> *Sign of Jonas,* 312

To say "I owe something to someone" makes many of us feel uncomfortable. It implies duty and dependency, obligation and weakness, conditions and constraints on our freedom to use our resources with responsible awareness of our debt. Indebtedness feels constrictive.

And yet what do we have that has not been given to us? Food on our table? It is the work of many human hands and earthly resources that produced it and enabled it to be transported to us. Our health? Our parents and our society have worked hard to provide the most reasonable environment for our healthy growth. Our ability to speak? Language has been given to us by forbears who structured it and taught it to us. All that helps us become more fully human has been transmitted to us by the gracious generosity of other human beings and ultimately a benevolent God. Even our faith in that God has been shaped by ancestors whose stories were spoken and written down that we might see life and meaning in a divine Presence in the world.

The flip side of indebtedness is gratitude. We are interdependent creatures as human beings. As a species, we lack the instincts to help us survive as infants and must depend on the human community and its traditions to teach us how to live. Socially and spiritually, we require the guidance of others. Yes, we are indebted. We can respond to that debt with an attitude of gratitude.

Gratitude is founded on humility. The word *humility* comes from the root word *humus*, or earth. Earth is the humble origin of humanity. We have the awesome ability to reflect on our origins and our relationship with the world, others, and God, an ability which is gift as well. Humility demands that I see myself as part of a larger matrix of existence, that I share in life because of others' contributions. Humility puts forth new eyes for me to see by and recognize "how much I owe everybody else."

In a large world, it is easy to overlook the interdependence of the human race. When my needs are met, I tend to take for granted the smooth flow of goods and services to my life. But once I embrace my humility as human, I must see that I am a member of a world population with its blessings and its blisters very much like my own. I am indeed responsible for others' survival, for traditions to be passed on, and for gratitude to be fostered. I am not a solitary citizen.

Humility helps us see our humanity, no more and no less ridiculous than the next person's. It can help us claim and aim our gratitude for all that has been given and all that we can give.

Blessed be the God and Father of our Lord Jesus Christ, who has blessed us in Christ with every spiritual blessing in the heavens....In him we have redemption by his blood, the forgiveness of transgressions, in accord with the riches of his grace that he lavished upon us.

EPHESIANS 1:3, 7-8

— 🌿 —

Gracious, Generous God, I owe you my breath, my heartbeat, my mind's activity. You are the Author of my being, the One who gives me life. I thank you for the multitudes of gifts you have showered on my existence and for each person who has played a role in my survival. Help me now to have clear eyes to see and accept my part in gracefully and humbly responding so that others might live too.

VIII. WORDS OF GOD

God Utters Me Like a Word

> "God utters me like a word containing a partial thought of Himself. A word will never be able to comprehend the voice that utters it."
>
> *New Seeds of Contemplation*, 37

As far as we know, only humans have the power of language. Language enables us to communicate with other humans, to form a verbal tradition with which to guide our offspring and to express the deepest needs of our heart. Language allows us to sing. A bit of ourselves goes with each word we utter, because it began in our own interior and thought processes. We can hurt with words, and we can heal with them.

God speaks a special language to us as human beings. Our Christian tradition speaks of God's revelation through the Word. This Word has been spoken in many ways. God reveals God's Self in a multitude of forms, including nature, history, people, and events. As Christians, we look to the Holy Bible for some of the stories of how God has revealed God's Self to us. God reaches out and tells us something about God's love and waits for the response of humanity. In other words, God utters a word to us. God initiates a dialogue, an invitation to enter into deepening relationship and engage with God's mystery.

If we hear the word God utters, we can respond. We can respond in faith through prayer, acts of justice, worship, and service. We can reply to God, using the words of our own unique personhood to say "Yes, I want to know you, Beloved. I reach back to YOU." Our very ability to say "Yes" is given by a God who hungers for relationship with us. It is the Word of God spoken in miniature into our fragile human hearts.

A dynamic between God's revolution and the response of humanity deepens with our consent. God speaks God's Word to our hungry hearts and we echo back our little words in response to God's beckoning. The Word of God meets the word of humanity, and the relationship between the two spirals deeper into intimacy.

Jesus Christ has been called the Word of God. Jesus Christ as the Word Incarnate, the Son of the Creator, is the fullest expression of both God's revelation and the human response of faith. Christ's Word shows us how to speak to the mystery of life, the Creator who first spoke. His Word is one of willing sacrifice as One who loves, laying down his life every day for the Lover. His voice is one of firmness and gentleness in leading us to speak our words of love too.

What is my word? What is my unique message in response to the God of revelation? How will my life be lived so that Love is known on the planet more completely? Though my voice is sometimes cross, my word is not erased. The forgiving God teaches me to speak again and invites me to join my efforts with those of others who seek to serve God. My voice again gets uttered within the voice of the One who uttered me. Even if I stutter, I am still uttered.

I will never know fully who it is that calls to me. I do not have to know. I only have to listen to that Word of God in each daily voice around me and choose how to respond. I am a little word within the great Voice. I am happy to sing my song as long as the One who loves chooses to direct me. Though only "a partial thought of himself," I have an important word to speak to continue the revelation of God and the response of humanity. Let my voice rise like incense in the evening offering.

> For just as from the heavens
> > the rain and snow come down
> And do not return there
> > till they have watered the earth,
> > making it fertile and fruitful,
> Giving seed to him who sows
> > and bread to him who eats,
> So shall my word be
> > that goes forth from my mouth;
> It shall not return to me void,
> > but shall do my will,
> > achieving the end for which I sent it.
>
> Isaiah 55:10-11

O Word That Is God, let your Word fall on the fertile ground of my heart. Let your voice be the voice that I hear in the night and at my earliest rising. Let my hands do the work of your hands as my little word speaks out its delight. I want to be a joyful sound in your ear. I want my "Yes" to be the deepest consent to all you have in mind for me.

We Are Words of His

> "Contemplation is...the response to a call; a call from Him Who has no voice, and yet Who speaks in everything that is, and Who, most of all, speaks in the depths of our own being: for we ourselves are words of His."
>
> *New Seeds of Contemplation*, 3

Sometimes we find ourselves desiring a clear answer from God about our lives and our decisions. It would be so much easier if God would give us direct signs or speak to us verbally about the direction that is best for our lives. We vaguely sense "a call" that moves us to respond in some way to a mysterious bidding. But because this call is not articulated in decipherable words, we are uncomfortable. Faith is demanded here. It is not easy to make life choices or begin new patterns based solely on a "feeling" that we are indeed being invited to change but lacking a precise confirmation.

How does the voiceless One speak? The One without words uses the many "words" of creation to speak to our heart. These "words" are not usually as dramatic and clear as we would like. They may be muffled by our own inner noise or by the congestion of the world. In the story of Elijah, God's voice was not in the thunder or the earthquake or the fire; God's voice was in the tiny whispering sound. (See 1 Kings 19:9-13.) What surprising humility our God has! God uses the unspoken desires of our heart or the whispers that only a quieted spirit can perceive to teach us the way for our lives. God uses gentle means to speak as the voiceless One.

Yet the beauty of this quiet approach is in its versatility. Every aspect of creation becomes a mouthpiece for the God who would speak. Every created being bears with it a word that can lead us to the Creator. It may be a word of inspiration, of invitation, or of initiation into a deeper relatedness with God.

Our spirit must become hushed to attend to the Word that is being spoken in the whispers. A certain discipline is required of us to prepare an interior disposition that is desirous and ready to hear such a soft spoken word. Our hunger must lead us into silence. It is our hunger to know that disposes us for the Word. It is also this hunger that marks us for life as the bearers of the Word.

Our own unique passion for the God who must speak leads us to speak on this God's behalf. We are compelled to speak of the passion we experience in contemplation; to share the Word as it is proclaimed to us in our own remarkable way. Our voice may be a whisper. It may be an ecstatic shout or a lyric song. It may change its timbre and tone as we grow in maturity and intimacy with God, swelling or softening in keeping with God's movement in us.

We become words of this God who must speak. We become new incarnations of the One who bears the name of Christ, the Anointed One. We carry the Word within us and speak from that authority when we honor the Word as it is spoken in the whispers of contemplation.

> One day to the next conveys that message;
> > one night to the next imparts that knowledge.
> There is no word or sound;
> > no voice is heard;
> Yet their report goes forth through all the earth,
> > their message, to the ends of the world.
> > > PSALM 19:3-5

— 🌿 —

Speak, Lord, your servant is listening...listening for the tiny voice of your fidelity, your desire for me. I listen with the ears of my body but more so with the ears of my heart, which seeks a confirmation of your creative direction for my life. I, too, want to speak but feel too young, too vain, too ignorant, too confused. Teach me your Word, O Lord, the one you want my life to speak...and let the earth become a word that whispers in my ear of your infinite benevolence.

IX. GOD'S WILL

God's Will

> "If you want to know what is meant by 'God's will' in man's life, this is one way to get a good idea of it. 'God's will' is certainly found in anything that is required of us in order that we may be united with one another in love."
>
> *New Seeds of Contemplation,* 76

"God's will" is often seen as a relatively exclusive directive for someone's life. Sometimes we think of God's will as a master plan ordained on high that is to govern our lives specifically, direct us in making choices, and keep us "safe" from any overt harm. Somehow, if we follow this will, we will be protected from all sorts of encounters and realities that could lead us into danger.

Is there perhaps a strain of isolationism in this? Are we not seeking some kind of assurance that we are on the right path and, therefore, need not receive any new challenges that could move us in some other direction? Maybe there is a less passive way to look at God's will.

God's will leads us into a direct encounter with our brothers and sisters in their multitude of needs. It's not always comfortable or safe. It is rarely predictable. God's will demands our response regardless of our vocational choice, our family size, or our work agenda. God's will is charity that offers itself spontaneously without paternalism, protection, or pride.

God's will demands that I love the person directly in front of me NOW. Love may have many faces. True love is a disciplined, deliberate, and delightful expression of concern and attentiveness. It means that we stop in our tracks to focus on the need in front of us, expressed in the feebleness of another being. We are disciplined to choose God's will through habitual acts of love for those requiring it of us. These daily acts of love lead us into unity with those whom God sends us.

God's will is not a solitary call. Rather, it is a call to solidarity with the one or the many who can daily lead us into generosity of heart. Their requests for love require our response and gradually deepen our sense of union with them and with God. We begin to think in unison with God, who offers us through these repeated surprises the opportunity for connectedness. God's will unites us.

When we carefully look at our own lives, where can we surprise God today with our willing response to those in need? How can we increase our spontaneous assent to God's will through an attitude of willing availability to the many little needs presented to us by others today? Can we begin to see and take delight in the splendid and playful unfolding of God's will in each person who reaches out to us?

In the daily choices about God's will, let us choose love. It will lead us back into relationship with one another as it leads us into greater oneness with the mind of God.

"And who is my neighbor?"

"The one who treated him with mercy."

"Go and do likewise."
LUKE 10:29, 37

— 🌿 —

Lord God, I want to know your will and then to feel the freedom that flows from following it. If your will is to lead me into love, I know I must embrace the challenges that my encounters invite me to. I must receive my neighbor in all the surprising ways my neighbor is presented to me. That's hard for me. Interruptions are hard for me. Help me to find delight in responding with mercy and to find the freedom that comes within that.

By Accepting All Things

> "...by accepting all things from Him I receive His joy into my soul, not because things are what they are but because God is Who He is, and His love has willed my joy in them all."
> *New Seeds of Contemplation*, 18

Each day we are given numerous opportunities to reinforce our faith in God. We are given delights when we have eyes to see them that remind us of God's magnanimity in caring for us. The triumphs of our day support our conviction that God wants good for us and is cordially showering us with success.

But what about the tragedies and difficulties in life? Are these not equally signs of God's presence in our lives? Are these not invitations to a deepening of relationship with the Mystery within all aspects of life?

Perhaps it is easier to identify God's concern for us in the warmth of the sun than in the cold of the rain. But God can feed us in the hunger of fasting as well as in the satisfaction of feasting. God attempts to introduce new freedom to us by aligning our choices with God's will, even in the struggles. Each of us grows in this intimacy with God when we desire the will of God without stipulations on how that will be lived out. Greater freedom is experienced when our food is the will of God, regardless of our preferences for the way God gives it.

Suddenly, God as God's Self in relation to us takes on greater importance than the way God's gifts are offered. The chief concern becomes not pleasure or pain, success or failure, but God's love for us behind all that is given. Our life is found in God's love and in accepting the diversity of forms that God uses to wean us from our own preferences in order to draw us into deeper fidelity and freedom.

Our acceptance of God's will for us gives us a new level of joy within this freedom. Our consent to God's movement in our lives, embracing more willingly and gladly all that God is using to draw us to God's mystery, increases God's love in our heart. We move in greater intensity to become who God is, love. We become the unique expression of that love God has ordained us to be from our very inception.

No matter what God gives, we receive it, and we do so gladly with the freedom that all that is given is for the advancement of love in our lives and in our world. Of course, we will continue to enjoy most fully that which is pleasurable to us as human beings. But that which is painful takes on new potential. We learn to receive both pain and pleasure with equal reverence for the God who is behind all of it. We increasingly seek the Giver, regardless of the gift.

This is the freedom and joy of living in the will of God. Our minds are altered gradually by both sun and rain, pleasure and pain, to see the Author who leads us into mystery. We begin to live in greater detachment no matter what is given because we seek God for who God is, no matter how that love is given.

When I think of you upon my bed,
> through the night watches I will recall
That you indeed are my help,
> and in the shadow of your wings I shout for joy.
My soul clings fast to you;
> your right hand upholds me.

PSALM 63:7-9

God Who Is Love, I am not always fond of your love given in trials, but I know your face is there. I seek your will in my life, even though at times I may hesitate in my willingness to undergo the darkness and rain that you may use to wean me from my own designs. I want you more than the pleasure and success I sometimes hunger for. Wean me gently from the protection I use to hang on to my own preferences and bring me according to your pace into greater freedom in relationship with you.

X.
LOVE IS A FOUNDATION

All Divided Worlds in Christ

> "If we want to bring together what is divided, we can not do so by imposing one division upon the other or absorbing one division into the other. But if we do this, the union is not Christian. It is political, and doomed to further conflict. We must contain all divided worlds in ourselves and transcend them in Christ."
>
> *CGB*, 21

The word *solidarity* has a political tone to it. Many of us associate it with the Polish sociopolitical resistance to Communist control. Yet there is a broader way to understand the term if we look at it from a Christian perspective. It involves recognizing the solitariness of each person, community, and nation but calls for a unity of spirits within this diversity. Christian solidarity solidifies human energies under one head, Christ's, and we see ourselves from a new humility with Christ as the mirror.

There is no doubt that division is innate to our world. Divisions emerge in part because of the diversity human beings bring to the world. This diversity is part of the richness of human complexity. Climate, history, and religious insight demand creative adaptation within the many communities of the human family. Multitudes of customs, stories, rituals, and guidelines emerge as each community forms a peculiar system of survival to instruct succeeding generations. Each tradition has its own unique merit and worth. Originally, there were logical reasons for the development of certain customs that those of other traditions often have difficulty understanding or relating to.

The diversity of cultures and traditions becomes more apparent as we proceed through the information age. Suddenly, cultures are rubbing shoulders with one another and not feeling completely compatible with the interchange. Healthy diversity is replaced by protective division.

Our legislators, heads of state, and international negotiators struggle to bring peace between the plurality of approaches to living on the planet. They try peace treaties, embargoes, sanctions, and boycotts to move the differing parties into compliance. Political means are only a beginning toward resolving the serious tensions that emerge within a pluralistic world. They will be short-lived because they are based on an imposition of law rather than on a free choice of the heart.

Merton reminds us that each of us individually is a world unto ourselves with many internal divisions. Daily we experience conflicts within ourselves that indicate the plurality of influences that have shaped our lives. Sometimes the peace within is merely tolerant coexistence rather than genuine harmony. Until we recognize the fragmentation within ourselves, the plurality of conflicting concerns that divide us internally, we will remain distant from a more global solution for the world's difficulties.

When it comes to solidarity, we must first see that all large-scale divisions are macrocosmic reflections of the microcosmic divisions inside. Wherever we see greed, loneliness, defensiveness, or pride, we see ourselves. Solidarity means recognizing the divided world in our own solitary existence, embracing it, and beginning the healing in our own inner house. Christ can serve as the model and mirror that heals us individually and teaches us how to mend our broken world.

> "The Advocate, the holy Spirit that the Father will send in my name—he will teach you everything and remind you of all that [I] told you. Peace I leave with you; my peace I give to you. Not as the world gives do I give it to you. Do not let your hearts be troubled or afraid."
>
> John 14:26-27

— 🍃 —

To the One Who Unites All Divisions, I know the feebleness of my own misery writ large in the wars, competition, and resistance among nations. I also know the triumph of love in my life, equally visible in walls coming down, in help being offered, and in heroic, humble compassion for the abandoned. For that which is lonely, forgotten, unfed, angry, or divided within me and my world, I ask your forgiveness and your aid.

Purity of Heart

> "The contemplative is not isolated in himself, but liberated from his external and egotistic self by humility and purity of heart—therefore there is no longer any serious obstacle to simple and humble love of other men."
>
> *New Seeds of Contemplation,* 66

The movement in prayer by the contemplative is a paradoxical one. On one hand, the contemplative journey into the interior of one's being takes one on a seemingly solitary path inward, circling down through all of one's shortcomings, strengths, blindnesses, and beauty to the core of one's full self. It appears to be an act of isolation, but the contemplative must descend into that "mixed bag" of humanness and identify and accept and be purged of the egoism that is part of being human. The contemplative recovers the humility and purity of the original self in the eye of God, replacing the "I" of their egoism. This frees them from their own preoccupations with self-sought sanctity and self-image.

In that still center where the most profound intimacy with God is experienced, a surprising occurrence takes place. That place which is most private becomes an ecstatic meeting ground for all humanity. An "implosion" of sorts occurs when the energy of the inner connectedness with God explodes into a radical sense of relatedness with all people.

Freed from the constraints of their own preoccupations, a new freedom is unleashed. Suddenly, in this inmost space, they feel a new innate and powerful sense of intimacy with the human family. They identify with the struggle of human hearts to deal with their own sinfulness in its many forms. They have looked at the difficulty of their own journey and seen it nakedly for what it was, a delicate journey in relationship with God that slowly weaned them from their solitary concerns.

And who, then, can judge? A human heart that has looked closely into its own harshness, unforgiveness, belligerence, and pain cannot easily throw stones at another who struggles with the same dilemmas. Here, true love can be born between human beings. Love has a chance. The contemplative simply and humbly accepts and receives the full gamut of human involvements and is invested with a new capacity to love the human persons wrestling with life. The obstacles of one's own judgmentalness, superiority, or humiliation are melted away by the contemplative's own purifying journey to the center, where all people dwell humbly at the feet of God.

Therefore, the contemplative uses her or his own life and prayer journey as a vehicle for transcending the self, a means to connect with all who share human flesh and desire the sacred, whether one admits it or not. The contemplative becomes able to love in a whole new way, not a way of personal effort but inspired by divine infusion. She or he will continue to live the struggle on a daily basis with difficult human beings but will be connected on a new level that frees her or him to be love from a different Source.

> "I pray not only for them, but also for those who will believe in me through their word, so that they may all be one, as you, Father, are in me and I in you, that they also may be in us, that the world may believe that you sent me. And I have given them the glory you gave me, so that they may be one, as we are one, I in them and you in me, that they may be brought to perfection as one...."
>
> JOHN 17:20-23

Source of All Love, the contemplative journey is a hard one, both alluring and alarming. I don't always have the courage to continue moving toward you in intimacy. The cost seems so high. But I know true love will only come with that purity of heart at the center, where you will erupt in me with new power and vitality. Keep me ready for the process, and fire my heart when it grows faint. Thank you for planting this seed of desire for you in my heart, Beloved, and give me strength for the journey.

Witness to the Nature of Love

> "Christ as man chose the way of total poverty, humiliation, self-emptying since in this way He was most completely identified with man, and also most freely witnessed to the nature of love as supreme freedom—a freedom that is not limited or stayed even by death."
> *Conjectures of a Guilty Bystander*, 342

A human person is a being who can choose fullness in many forms. Fullness can be experienced as an accumulation of resources that protect us from the poverty of want. Or fullness can be an egoic filling up of our functional identity that shields us from defeat and the pain of self-emptying.

However, a paradoxical fullness is also experienced in the exclusively human ability to surrender to the need of another and in this emptiness find unlimited freedom. This fullness is more difficult to choose willingly, but human beings have the capacity and the spiritual foundations for such a puzzling fullness. What is this spiritual foundation?

It is love. Love has a human face as well as a divine one. It is this potential toward love in the human being that God chose to enter into and therefore reveal a new fullness to the world. God chose to identify with our relatively fragile species because the human being can most suitably witness to the dramatic freedom within love.

But this fullness of freedom would require the seemingly contrary movement toward humility. The fullness of God would manifest itself in the impoverished nature of humanity, funneling as much of God's divine power as was possible into human form. Then, within the limitations of human flesh, God would empty God's Self through human death, a death imposed by human brothers and sisters. But love would be the significant element that made this self-emptying valid. The pouring out of God's love through a human form would unleash a new belief, a new power, in the human person that could not be limited or held down—even by bodily death.

A new freedom to choose life in a radically different way was introduced through Jesus' humanness. Love anchored this choice to a God that far transcended human limitation. However, the potential of humanity was transformed dramatically because Christ chose freely the weak human form with which to identify. Through his self-emptying, we as human beings learned a new fullness and witnessed a freedom in which we could participate.

The nature of love does not allow it to be stayed by death or limited by a life span. Christ introduced the paradox of surrender as a means to fullness and freedom. He identified with our weakness and saw within it a fertile field for expanded freedom. God chose to mirror for us our own potential through poverty, humility, and self-emptying by using the image of Christ to bring us to ourselves.

Have among yourselves the same attitude
that is also yours in Christ Jesus,
Who, though he was in the form of God,
did not regard equality with God
> something to be grasped.
Rather, he emptied himself,
taking the form of a slave,
coming in human likeness,
and found human in appearance,
he humbled himself,
becoming obedient to death,
> even death on a cross.
Because of this, God greatly exalted him....
>> PHILIPPIANS 2:5-9

— ❦ —

Free Spirit of Christ, I stand overwhelmed with the challenge of love. I cannot love so freely, and yet I desire to freely give and surrender somehow to this paradox of fullness. Teach me to choose the loving approach to the world, that gradually I may be emptied in order to be filled by you. Help me taste the freedom that will move me to desire to love as you have loved.

Love Is My True Identity

> "Love is my true identity. Selflessness is my true self. Love is my true character. Love is my name."
>
> *New Seeds of Contemplation*, 60

Who am I before the face of God? What am I known as? How will God define me as unique and yet as one with all? What is my significant feature in the mind of God?

I am the remarkable expression of a unique form of love that God gives to the world. Love is the true identity that I struggle to realize, somehow customized in my creation to be revealed in a profoundly different way from the love of anyone else. Love is my real nature. I will only know my true self in the gradual revelation of love that is specific to me. God will know my voice and recognize me through the gentle incarnation of love that is God's truth inside me.

Love takes on a fresh form in my slow discovery of self. As I share that with the world, my true character emerges. It comes forth through some toil in the self-revelation process. I learn about my true self through growth in selflessness, where I abandon myself and my persistent personal agendas for a greater need and purpose. I develop character lines that shape the contour of my true face, weathered by life but full of wisdom.

Love looks different on me. It shows itself within the daily choices, sacrifices, acts of freedom, and mistakes that I make. My story is made up of many twists and turns that challenge the peculiar refinement of love within me. It is not always clear how love lives in me, but with each breath of the Spirit love has potential. I can choose love, and even if I live it clumsily and ambiguously, God honors my choice to love as valuable and valid. My success at love is not my true identity. My sincerity at struggling to love is my great advocate.

So love is my name. Could I have any other name when I am created in the image and the likeness of a God who is love? Could any other approach to life really honor the magnitude of my being if it is not rooted in love? I think not. Love is my core. I care about my world, my life, my God. Love is the nature of who I am.

Therefore, handle carefully the time you have with me on the earth. And I promise you this. I will handle with care the face of love I see in you. For love is your true identity too. You will embrace the world differently from me, but love is your origin and your true form. I respect that unique nuance of love that is yours, and I ask that you see mine, even though at times both of us will find our eyesight blurred by human lack of love.

Take your love seriously, and take mine equally so. And yet in those times of dissonance between us, remember that our differences are bound up in one love, which unites and reconciles all divisions. Let love be that which binds us yet also distinguishes the extraordinary flow of God's energy within us.

> If there is any encouragement in Christ, any solace in love, any participation in the Spirit, any compassion and mercy, complete my joy by being of the same mind, with the same love, united in heart, thinking one thing.
>
> PHILIPPIANS 2:1-2

— ❦ —

Great Love of the Universe, I am yours; you are mine. Together we breathe love into the world in a way that is amazingly alive. I need you, dear One, to keep me faithful to the revelation of love within me. I need the love of my brothers and sisters to complement my contribution of compassion to the world. Let my eyes never grow dim in perceiving your love within the human family, and help me to reverence the many forms of love that struggle to unveil themselves in the world.

www.ingramcontent.com/pod-product-compliance
Lightning Source LLC
Chambersburg PA
CBHW071624170426
43195CB00038B/2097